OCCASIONAL remedies

Poems by John Fox

First published 2024 by IRON Press
5 Marden Terrace
Cullercoats
North Shields
NE30 4PD
tel +44(0)191 2531901
ironpress@xlnmail.com
www.ironpress.co.uk

ISBN 9781-838344-4-8-1
Printed by Imprint Digital

© The poems and drawings, John Fox
© This collection, IRON Press

Cover and book design, Brian Grogan and Peter Mortimer
Clown puppet by John Fox

Typeset in Georgia 10pt

IRON Press books are distributed by
NBN International
and represented by Inpress Ltd
Milburn House, Dean Street
Newcastle upon Tyne NE1 1LF
tel: +44(0)191 2308104
www.inpressbooks.co.uk

BORN IN HULL 1938. ARTIST-POET & STREET BAND MUSICIAN. With Sue Gill and others co-founded the legendary celebratory arts company Welfare State International (WSI) 1968-2006.www.welfare-state.org. Archived WSI in 2006. Started Dead Good Guides (DGG) www.deadgoodguides.co.uk to seek a role for art that weaves itself fully into the fabric of our lives. DGG trains secular celebrants, offers practical workshops, readings and is creating *Wildernest*, a sanctuary beach garden by Morecambe Bay.

Fox and Gill advocate art that generates imaginative wonder and continuing participation. Their key pioneering work in Ulverston, Cumbria (now "The Festivals Town") features the much copied Lantern Parade (from 1984) a Flag Fortnight, Fine Fest and Lanternhouse. WSI's extensive archive is in the Theatre Collection at Bristol University where The Wellcome Trust is funding preservation and accessibility.

Selected exhibitions.
1993 Permanent woodcut triptych in foyer of Trinity Enterprise Centre, Barrow.
2008 Mid Pennine Arts. *Radical Mayhem*.
2011 Brantwood, Coniston. *Fragments from the Weather Station*.

Selected awards.
1991 and 1998 Northern Electric Arts.
2006 Arts Council England, Life Time Achievement.
2012 MBE.
2017 Cumbria Life: Mary Burkett (with Sue Gill).

Academia.
1959-63 Ruskin School of Drawing, Oxford.
1963-67 Fine Art. Newcastle University.
1967-70 Librarian Bradford School of Art.
1970-74 Senior Lecturer in Fine Art Leeds Polytechnic.
Honorary Fellow of Universities of Cumbria and Central Lancashire.
Companion of Liverpool Institute of Performing Arts.

Writing
Publications listed on p52.
Magazines: The Fire Crane, The Robin Hood Book. Iron Magazine (Issue 78). Plus...

Music.
Soprano sax. 25 years with Blast Furness, 20 strong street band.
Melodeon and accordion with Fox Family Band.
Songwriter. (Foxy's Songbook)

The Best Bit
Married to Sue Gill for six decades.
Living by the sea in *The Beach House*, a wooden home on stilts with grass roof.
Two gifted adult children, namely Dan inventor, musician, Hannah animateur, performer and image maker.
Five amazing grandchildren aged 10 to 24.

JOHN FOX MBE
DEAD GOOD GUIDES
www.deadgoodguides.co.uk
www.welfare-state.org

The Poems

VANMAN	9
40 YEARS A WELDER	10
NO IDEA OF WHAT	11
HOLD TIGHT	12
TAXIDERMIST	13
TRILOBITE	14
MOON BALLOON	16
NO RETURN	17
QUARRYMAN	18
SANDWICH OF GRIEF	20
RADIOTHERAPY - MRI SCAN	21
RANDOM	22
TURTLE TURTLE	23
FOREVER WINE	24
CINEMA	26
EXPECTATIONS	27
BILL'S WAKE	28
MOTORHOME	30
UNDERNEATH	31
FOX	32
SLIPPED MY MIND	33
IRON AGE FORT	34
A POINT OF VIEW	36
IN PRAISE OF IDLENESS IN TAVIRA	37
PRAYING TO OUR BOOTS	38
TAKE THESE CHAINS	39
ROARING	40
HOWLING IN MAJORCA	41
DIBBING FOR VICTORY	42
WALKING THE WOLDS WAY	43
NO SHOW	44
SALMON	45
GIACOMETTI GIRL	46
SPIDER	47
HOLIDAY BARN	48
BEACHED WHALE	49
COACH TRIP TO THE VOLCANO	50

John Fox Writes

I am given to spectacle.

With Welfare State International WSI (1968-2006) and our big fire-shows, pyrotechnics, site specific theatre, lantern parades and imaginative excess, we were shameless exhibitionists. However in Toronto in 1981 Ken Feit, a peripatetic Jesuit story teller, explained that while WSI engineered "explosions" he generated "implosions", immediately firing up a single grain of popcorn in a teaspoon of olive oil held over a candle flame.

So my poems are wordy implosions. Unexpected pinprick observations. Tiny found stories. Sometimes fearful, melancholic, playful, angry or mysterious, I am never sure where understandings come from, but they can hold surprising revelations. Tiny things can be wondrous and terrifying …
like the fierce jaws of a minute ragworm under an electronic microscope. But also, like a wart on a crocodile, the microcosm can lurk in a massive macrocosm.

Such prompts can shift consciousness, bundling together evolution, history, news, memory, sentiment into a heady synthesis. A necklace of images, luminous baubles tied together in reflective and meditative mode. A diary, to digest and connect with forgotten stepping stones.

That's all about me of course. But what of the reader? Why should this sieving process from an odd octogenarian showman be of the slightest interest to anyone else? I just hope that these idiosyncratic wanderings, can lift a particular note to a universal chord. All to wish for. Big and little and big in the little.

A flight from spectacle maybe.

December 2023

VANMAN

White-van man, stressed
to the bone by tachometers
and profit drones,
is satnav-ed to oblivion.
Just dropping.

No place to turn round.
A dead end.
Don't know how to get out.
I bet you just chill out here,
on the beach, listening to the sea.

Any chance he could stop
on his way back?
Look at the horizon for five minutes?
Go by Roy's ice cream van.
Park by the sea.
Roy was once a coal man.
Now does a good chocolate chip.

No. No time.
120 drops a day.
I hate my job.
And if I stop to look at the sea
I'll chuck myself in.

40 YEARS A WELDER
For George

When you are well
- which you will be -
sunbeams on steel will be sunbeams once again.
Your saxophone will gleam, dusted off at last.

Once more
your head will jump back
to relish break dancing at dawn
(when it's OK to be upside down).
Then all those mis-threaded screws
will pop out and back.
Stand, rustless, to salute you in a shiny guard of honour,
shouting:

40 years is enough. 40 is enough.

Your suit of stale armour will disintegrate.
Its dust forming a vapour trail,
soft as new gauze on an old wound.

When you are well
- which you will be -
on the drive to work
traffic cones will dance the Boogie.
Tarmac will melt into a cool lagoon
and cat's eyes will shine.

Goodbye to The Daily Shift/Shaft.

NO IDEA OF WHAT

Outside the curtains
a full tide
pounds and scours,
throwing up offerings.

Friday's sheep, washed up,
is frothing with worms.
Bruised and decayed,
carved with ochre ravines,
neck thrusting and segmented.

Time for dog walkers
to clutch their spaniels.
Time for contractors
to bury another carcass.

Space to contemplate a spiral of rooks,
locked in blackened gossip.
Space to peruse the evening tide.
To wait. To wait,
with no idea of what -
between a kipper box and a drowning -
might next be laid.

HOLD TIGHT

On the cliff, gorse, cadmium yellow,
flings silks into a gunmetal sky.
Rising and thrusting. No vapour trails.
Stillness. A symphonic Spring.

Tonight the indigo black slab
of a granite sea lies in waiting.
Waiting for street lights across the Bay to go out,
like eleven thousand dead from Covid by today. *

Hold one pink crab shell,
skeletal jewel from seaweed mountain.
Hold it tight, for a moment,
as nightfall blankets footfall
and the sea reclaims the beach.

* *14 April 2020*

TAXIDERMIST

In her grey tray of wings,
clipped from fallen birds,
she sprinkles borax
to eternalize
goldfinch, blue tit, thrush and hawk.

With tweezers and sable brush
she plucks feathers.
Binds them with oiled twine,
layer by layer, bone to bone,
filigree to filigree.

Her oil lamp splutters.
A soft flame glows lilac,
illuminating the intangibility of lost birds
fluttering over the ivory edge.

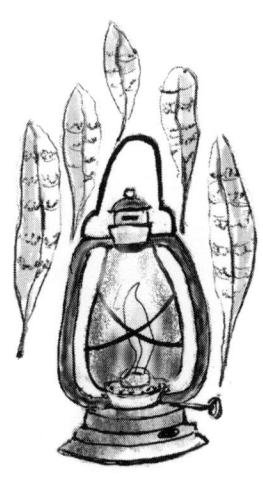

TRILOBITE

Trillions of them, alive.
Furtling for aeons
in fissured seas,
carpeting the planet
before carpets were the thing.
All gone.
No good wishing
those scores of woodlice
under every stump
are the same. They're not.

Trilobite fossils are common,
even the spiny ones
with lobster periscopes
and curly slater legs.
The best ones fetch a bit.
Such chunky logic
of segmented form
is indispensable
for polished paperweights
on mahogany desks.

Our ancestors knackered out.
Like us, when comes the day,
genetically engineered
brainbots oust our flesh.
Share that thought
with Paraharpes*
on your desk
diligently holding down
desiccated leaves in the storm:
the insolvency audit
and that final bank demand.
Paraharpes winks in his perspex dome,
signalling what we already know.

*Paraharpes was a remarkable trilobite in which the general spines are prolonged into a 'brim' extending along its 5-6 cm length.
Richard Fortey. TRILOBITE! Eyewitness to Evolution.
Flamingo 2000.*

MOON BALLOON

This morning, moon driven, the raucous tide
swept all beach shingle aside,
ripping barnacles from driftwood laths
and dumping reeds on coastal paths.

Later, 'en famille' we trek to Moon Balloon
visitor attraction in the Coronation Ballroom.
Huge ladders cleared cobweb encrusted
chandeliers and cherubs all dusted.

Suspended, glowing, with NASA images
of scabby craters and volcanic ridges,
swaying, inflated, in a ghoulish light.
Infants below cartwheel in delight.

No notions here of a big green cheese
or Man in the Moon with eyebrows to please.
No gravitational pull. No tidal thunder,
yet still a place to stop and wonder.

Maybe in a moment a trapdoor will spring
spewing toads or an ET thing,
while a daisy cow jumps over the Lune
and a randy dish runs off with the spoon?

NO RETURN

Sea defences rear
slab upon slab of
sliced black rock.
Heaved and fragmented to
causeways of no return.

Boats once came. Trains once ran.
Walkers left. The space emptied.
With storm wracked fear
forked tempests
smashed his expectations.

Within his sight a solid branch
held out.
Within his sight, a single tree
held the rope.

He could hear the sea.

She put tulips on the earth below.
White petals nested into belonging
with celandines, wood anemones
and bluebells to thrust aside
daffodils frozen with death.

And the sea pounds still.

QUARRYMAN

When he split the stone
he found an angel.
A winged fossil grounded for
two million years.

No one believed him.
He gambled and drank.
In debt to publican, butcher and doctor
(who claimed the apparition as fee)
he cut his wrists with slate.
His heart a jagged crystal,
broken with light.

SANDWICH OF GRIEF

Sometimes, with sadness,
you have to grasp it.
Clasp it to your heart
and your belly.

    Waiters pass with
    trays of jolliness.
    The next table is
    raucous with replenishment.

        A friend died on Tuesday
        another one today.
        Make a sandwich of grief.
        hold it deep, raw, flattened,
        between, between.

            Hold it between
            and nurture emptiness
            in the stomach.

RADIOTHERAPY - MRI SCAN

Scared couples cling together,
holding hands to brave lino corridor,
to the distant Cellar of Lead,
Throne Room of Linear Accelerator Number One.

LA1 is an enamelled waltzer
white as porcelained bathrooms.

A fairground tumbril from Star Wars,
empty as last dance ballrooms.

LA1 rotates slowly round elongated flesh.
LA1 gyrates with slotted slabs in neon green.
Waiting, targeting, thrusting, piercing, bleeping
to find any lurking tumour.
To soften the gut
for keyhole surgery on Monday.

RANDOM

Driving from the petrol station
his car hit mine.
The air bag saved me.
Our VW written off.

I didn't see you, he said in court,
your car was black as the one behind.

Random.
Broken beak on an invisible window,
legs twitching to the sky.

Random.
Vulture sucked into jet over mountain peak.
Mudslide with bodies wrapped in plastic.
Reflecting sun blinded a careful driver.
A stick in the bike wheel.

Random.
Grandmother with three infants,
apron-stringed behind,
buying bread when the shrapnel fell.

Whoever designed that cluster bomb,
whoever steered the drone
went home after work.
No cocoa in the cupboard.
Sent his son to the corner shop,
bike bent,
legs twitching,
no one's fault.

Random.

TURTLE TURTLE

Over a marble sarcophagus
by a courtyard pool,
the invigilator
yawns away her morning shift.

The corpse has gone.

A Phoenician Queen is lost to
a palaeontologist's cabinet
somewhere in grimy Athens.
Here her empty coffin
fills the morning
with a remaindered hairband
and jars of rosemary embrocation.

So, one invigilator,
two Japanese students,
three Professors,
an anxious Curator
and us,
share weighty mysteries
with a turtle in the rain.

FOREVER WINE

On the rim of a twelfth century
museum bowl, worked in fire,
two young lovers pause.

Musicians and cooks, goats and sheep
lollop in procession round a well of wine.

In an adjacent cabinet
two ancient duck-billed oil lamps,
glued whole with restorer's clay,
revel with love and light.

Relics dutifully re-worked.
Preserved and annotated,
to underpin those glimmers
we share in the common dark.

CINEMA

She always goes to the pictures on Mondays.
It shortens the week.

Handbag with cans of G & T,
pocket of chocolate eclairs.
Unwrapping brings tutting
but no other threat.

I choose films with care.

'Judy' was a mistake though.
Rainbows soured with drugs and booze,
Yellow Brick Road tarred and ossified.
Dead at 47. Too close.

Eclairs melt, lacy,
like autumn leaves run over.

Slip out before the end.
Whisper away the cans.
Shove them, with love, into the bin provided.

EXPECTATIONS

She expected
Sauvignon chilled in crystal,
with napkins, starched and crisp.
She expected
magnolia promise,
with lunch on the terrace.
Instead he proffered
market trestles on tab-end cobbles.
House wine in polythene,
and pork scratchings in a plastic bag!
At least, he found the eco-bin
to toss the splattered tissues in.

BILL'S WAKE

In memoriam Bill Mitchell 1951 - 2017
Artistic Director of WILDWORKS

Over the dunes where the sea is at whirlpool frenzy
an Easterly gale shreds pirate flags.
Anchored below, a big marquee is buffeted white.
Full of warm beings who cosset and gossip
over theatrical tales of Bill who died,
age sixty five on Good Friday, three weeks ago.

This is tribe.

Someone pegged the tent.
Another guyed the flags.
Others did hot dogs and
plied Jacob's ladder with food galore.
As the band triggers nostalgia,
four generations create a layer cake
of site-specific love and belonging.

This is tribe.

Outside in the night, fierce lines of white bunting
flap like ghosts on parade.
No still point.
No still canvas
for Bill to paint a landscape show
or sketch more swirling scarlet cliffs.
Never to make another wild mark.

The screen on the tent wall bulges in the wind
holding Bill in a thousand powerpoint snaps
from childhood rocking horse to skyhook dominion.
Moments.   Moments.   Moments.
Held and gone.

This is tribe.

Looking back from the top edge of the night-time dunes
under a black moon over St Ives
the white marquee in the hollow below
could be a refugee camp
(Bill supported such concerns)
or a home-grown fairground laced with LED's.
Even a flyblown hospital from MASH.
Just now it is a cocoon of moments.
Holding and lifting Bill's tribe.

DANCING.

MOTORHOME

She fell in love with the eye level grill.
Upholstery was nearly new.
Nightlight, succulent pink
and curtains tangerine whoopydoo.

Chassis though was rusted through
and the cambelt buggered too.
Then, just before they stopped for bed,
pistons rammed the cylinder head.

Sixteen thousand pounds was a lot,
but cheaper than a building plot.
And that ventilator is a wonder.
All garlic smells cast asunder.

They pushed their dream to a lay-by free,
then searched for comforting SKY TV.
Wildlife films waiting to be seen
and in the fridge chocolate mint ice cream.

UNDERNEATH

Underneath was a boat.
Underneath the look-at-me towers of 9/11.
Those who dig and scrape
find a white oak frame.

Made from Philadelphian wood
this sloop of 1733 is fated to be embedded
with the burning girders
of a screwed awakening.
Easy to say its passengers then,
skilfully propelled over Manhattan waters,
had no idea of death by plane.

Their revolution, driven by
the trill of drum and bayonet,
was equally uncertain.

Uncertain as jet planes
navigating a launch of boils
from an adolescent bomber
certain of his hereafter.

Forever embedded in the same landfill,
false teeth, plastic cards, melted rings,
crushed cans and wandering strands of hair
are nudged by microbes to compost soil.

Memories are never merely ash.
Under so many ploughed earthworks
and collapsed ideals, ancient timbers wait.

FOX

A fox from Sea Wood
is dead on the road,
flattened to a membrane
over cat's eyes.

Last evening
fox leapt through nettles
to tear and eat
a rabbit at bay.

At moonrise
fox sprung across the road.
As before,
taut and certain.

At moonfall
fox was hit at speed
by an ordinary car
with a shiny bumper.

An hour ago
fox's soft blue belly
rose gleaming.
A hilllock levitating.

Now between traffic,
magpies viciously efficient,
pluck corrugations of skin.
Thinned to oblivion over cat's eyes.

SLIPPED MY MIND

These bones are too delicate to keep.
No place for them in our bird museum.

The corpse of the thrush,
concussed on the window,
is lying on the deck,
ready to chuck over the rail.
To compost or bury politely?

Slipped my mind.

Bone sticks remain.
Sternum to tibia.
Titanium white.

Scrape off any flesh glued down.
A credit card will do the job.

IRON AGE FORT

Under foot a dead sheep.
A cold heap. A sheared coat,
white and fading as melting snow.
Twin sockets nestle in her spine.
Bleeding binoculars drilled by crows
reveal where her kidneys were plucked out.

Stepping over rigid death
a green gate with stubborn hinge
leads us to scarred hollows on the brink
where Iron Age remnants crunch
into tufts of strident marsh grass,
speared red in the setting sun.

The same sun for us and for them.
A bullet star. A diadem.
Ice Age trees steaming on the northern edge
skins drying on a makeshift fence.
Rattle gun crow, same magpie of fate
still sucking kidneys on bog-bound slate.

A POINT OF VIEW

The beach mud is chunked up into slabs.
Chocolate fudge cake if you are so inclined
or trenches at Ypres if you look the other way.
Hard to accumulate a point of view.

The hissing of the incoming tide
undercurrents the cackle and ping
of birds. Mainly crows and rooks
flitting with worms between soil and nest.

The slabs are already underwater.
Gaze shifts. Oystercatchers pinprick to cloud.
Hawthorn blossom folds like clotted cream
next to elephantine trunks of ash.

A wagtail trips across pebble-dashed shells
tide-dumped on the coastal path.
Seething waves change gear to lap and suck,
to reveal within reeds - bayonet sharp - an upturned boat.

Blue as forget-me-knots. Blue as a corpse.
Curved like history, upside down.
Forgotten. Lurking. Not yet sunk
into deep mud, over a gangrene trench.

IN PRAISE OF IDLENESS IN TAVIRA

There is no doubt that next week,
back home, walking in the rain from Asda,
we will not pause by the river
to watch trout leap over one-clawed crabs.

There is no doubt that in November,
skating from Tesco on pavements of ice,
we will not linger in the park
to contemplate meringue finials in a cloudless sky.

There is no doubt that come December,
sheltering from sleet by the Aldi roundabout,
we will not loiter by the tumbling weir
singing Tom Waits from an old radio.

I'll love you 'til the wheels come off ...

No doubt whatsoever
that, one quiet morning, we will return,
to these mosaics on sand, their clock hands in the air.
To wonder why the seagulls here
(unlike ours at home)
do not gorge on refuse sacks,
or on takeaways exited in late night vomit.

PRAYING TO OUR BOOTS

Like old bones in a washing machine
we trundle through hedgerow tunnel,
through boulder alley, where flowing streams
once earned a waterwheel a living.

Stones clatter, clints rattle,
reluctant to harbour withered walking sticks
of wrinklies clinging to head high roots
tumbling on spongy lichened walls.

History is fly paper.
We oldies stick on for a tasty while,
fluttering our wings in delight and remembrance.
Praying to our boots that we arrive at the pub.

In the Sun Inn we laugh round our table
recalling a water wheel gentrified in cement.
Cosseting our flapjack of personal millstones.
Breeding, emerging, living, celebrating.

History is a table cloth,
tight as a drum. White, pure, crisp,
ready for tureen and crystal,
to splatter joyously in family feast.

Wedding anniversary. Job success.
Leaving high school. New house.

Everyone here from our loins.
We survived hedgerow tunnel,
saw iron age ghosts on Ingleborough top,
found a hare's nest on the bank of the Lune.

Outside, boulder stones rattle.
Inside, dust settles on our drum.
A carafe of wine breathes gently,
while at the window a miller's child taps to be let in.

TAKE THESE CHAINS

With a skinful of ale you can fall over the edge
into the grey and deepening Mersey.
And today the ferry is suspended.

The riverside walk is laced with padlocks
looped, holding, linked and locked,
rusty, polished, heartfelt and signed.

All mildewed yet glowing with eternal promises
from many a one night duet. Consummate
nuts and bolts of sentiment, longing and belonging.

Tonight we'll lock our door, drink a bevy,
renew the bus pass, play a vid or two
and look once more for the old hot water bottle.

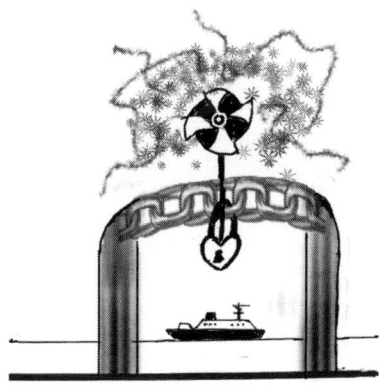

ROARING

I stand on a sandy beach
touched with the footprints of children,
who run like liquid hares
over and around and back.

Similar prints were in the Olduvai Gorge
and found after radiation in Hiroshima.

The roaring in the sky
could be a plane or an explosion.
Putin or Xi Jinping come to mind.

A notch away is another sound though.
A thin buffeting sigh.
An oak tree wind carrying fierce spores
is bounding over the endless perimeter fence.

The one the children are just beginning to climb.

HOWLING IN MAJORCA

On the Miro Terrace we savour art.
Reminisce on family, luck and legacy.
The barman says Miro had four grandchildren:
Two dead, one drunk, one Down's.

Across the road an air-conditioned tenement
ferments with draped windows and antennae.
The baby is howling to be fed.
Leaning through the open window
her brother is yelling into the warm night.
Yelling across the concrete courtyard.
Mama. Mama. Mama.
Just howling.

DIBBING FOR VICTORY

Take twenty sacks of crocus corms.
Hope for two thousand blooms.
Find a team of Sunday morning yawners
with spiky dibbers.
Add earth, kneeling mats, sunshine, banter and coffee.

Pierce ground, four inches down, drop in corm right way up.
Come spring, a purple mantle will carnival over rippled gold.

A motley trowelling by the residents.

You sold guns to Arabs.
She did botox on bums.
He reads the Daily Mail.
Your mother's a frequent flyer
AND a climate denier.
Your dog pissed on our geraniums.

Yet when we are all on our knees
penitents digging in cloistered marble,
we are saffron gatherers in a Minoan fresco,
peasants tossing hay in an impressionist dream.
Back then, time was music, politics dandruff
and any putative difference a mere scab to be tossed to the
wind.

NOTE: Crocus
Latin from Greek krokos, of Semitic origin, related to Hebrew
karkōm and Arabic kurkum.

WALKING THE WOLDS WAY

Dry valleys in silent scoops criss-cross
upturned shoulders of embroidered earth.
Death no longer crawls black on the bottom trail.
No plague village remains.
Except,
your eye may catch a weal of meadow grass
your toe a line of crushed flints or
elemental scars which spring a phantom cart,
sweet with bales of hay
or sour with shrouds sewn in haste.

As we backpack over buried cries,
observing ravenous butterflies
- jewelling on dung -
we trek on to the yellow parasol,
where pastries baked at dawn
glisten with fresh milk and clover honey
harvested on the same bottom trail.

NO SHOW

Out of season, the puppet theatre is empty.
A creaking booth.
Scenery rolled.
Microphone off.
Coconut hooves, battle clogs silent.

The tortoise encrusted with fake diamonds hibernates,
while the snare drum, frayed with string, is mildewed damp
and weighty knights, with woodworm,
lean their steeds under the sagging roof.
No show.

No show until the sun shines hot.
Until rats cease to gnaw the leather hinge
of the locked jaws of the wooden crocodile.
Then the pianola will strike up
a clattering carousel of dreams.

SALMON

In the mouth of the Tweed
five men in sand and tide
circle nets, herding salmon.
Each thump of a lump hammer
splatters brains to market gold.

Holding the hand of his grandchild
an old fisherman watches
as the whole sky becomes a dead fish,
silver and sliced, with sunset scales.

GIACOMETTI GIRL

In Memoriam Chris Bowler 20th May 2014.

There's a cobbled square in Holstebro
where a metal girl resides.
A Giacometti sculpture
most thin and rarefied.

She balances on an iron box
flat footed and a loner.
Plinth resting on little wheels
she's worth two million krone.

The citizens of Holstebro
love art of every kind,
though two million extra krone
concentrates the mind.

She's very still this little girl,
with no childish dreams,
for she's bolted into concrete
watched by police in teams.

Tragically, historically
she lost her innocence.
Corrupted by investment
in a world that makes no sense.

Three feisty women descend upon
the lonely statuette,
with welding torch and goggles.
Soon bronze begins to melt.

Smoke obscures the cameras
lined up in the sky,
where Giacometti girl
is soon to dance and fly.

She skips away - a fairy tale!
Then spins up to the moon,
as two million Danish krone melt,
in Holstebro at noon.

SPIDER

You folded instantly
like a camp-stool with woodworm.
Squashed by accident.
Knotted, knuckled, gone.
An impossible tiny ball living
suspended on hundred metre legs.
No evident reason for being
except to appear every morning
on our bathroom wall with nothing to eat.
I hope there are more of you,
to blow on gently while I shave.

HOLIDAY BARN

The oil cloth on our table
shines with the icons of
farmyard beasts.
Watercoloured neat.

A sepia cow,
a magenta cockerel,
a duck - Beatrix white -
and a lamb, pebble-dashed cream,
nestled into honeysuckle blooms
under marigold moons.

Off the stove
onto a slatted tray
scalding coq-au-vin
bubbles in Beaujolais.

A fountain of juicy fowls
offers succulent grease
to us munching human beasts.
No uproar. No war. No wrath.

BEACHED WHALE

Seventy years old
forty-five feet long.
Gulf streamed from Florida
to die in Morecambe Bay.

On pilgrimage we gawped.
Risking quicksand
in the wrong shoes
on the wrong legs
to pay homage
to your magnificence.

Inflated with stench.
Maggots in your mouth,
fins ripped by dogs,
plastic bottles in your eyes.

Buried in a pit.
You arrived like an upturned boat
ribbed in golden sun.
A year on we dug you up.
Resurrected. Bleached.
A flotilla of bones
resplendent in a museum roof.
Worth another gawp.

COACH TRIP TO THE VOLCANO

*Montanas del Fuego, Timanfaya National Park, Lanzarote
March 2015.*

Piloted by an earthling
we veer out in a charabanc
banging over million years of lava,
circum-ventilating a throbbing cadaver,
scabbed and treacled with blackened teeth.

Levitating the hairpins of Valkyrie
our bus swings through the bowels of eternity
and stratified brochures of tourist delight.

From a plummeting eye socket a cinder blinks.
A smitch of fresh grass fluoresces adolescent green,

while the driver stops for a fag.

Other Publications with words and images by John Fox can be purchased via Paypal from:
www.deadgoodguides.co.uk

Manuals and Handbooks
Engineers of the Imagination: Methuen. Welfare State International (WSI). Coult and Kershaw. 1983/1990

Eyes on Stalks. Methuen. Personal account of WSI with drawings. John Fox. 2002

The Dead Good Time Capsule Book. Ed. Gill Gill. 1999

The Dead Good Funerals Book. Sue Gill, John Fox. 1996/2004

The Dead Good Book of Namings & Baby Welcoming Ceremonies. Ed. J.How. with Sue Gill. 1996/2004

Dead Good Guides, with Sue Gill and Gilly Adams, offer two four day courses every year on the nuts and bolts of personal and secular ceremonies for Rites of Passage. For further information: www.deadgoodguides.co.uk

Poetry and Essays
Matey Boy: **IRON Press.** Epic poem by Kevin Fegan. Linoprints John Fox. 1991

Ground: Poems, woodcuts and linocuts. Ed. Gilly Adams. 1998

You Never Know. Poems. John Fox 2011/2022

The Rain Days. Poems. John Fox 2021

Foxy's Song Book. 50 songs. Lyrics: John Fox. Scores: Fleming, D. Fox, Hamilton, Howarth, Mishalle, Moser, Stephens, Westbrook. 2021

In All My Born Days. Sue Gill 2021

Eighty-Something, a lifetime of conversation. Sue Gill and John Fox. 2023